#DoBetter
Move Beyond Fear and Procrastination in 21 Days

Dawniel P. Winningham

BK Royston Publishing
P. O. Box 4321
Jeffersonville, IN 47131
502-802-5385
http://www.bkroystonpublishing.com
bkroystonpublishing@gmail.com

© Copyright – 2016

All Rights Reserved. No part of this book may be reproduced, stored in a retrieval system, or transmitted by any means without the written permission of the author.

Cover Design: Bill Lacy Graphics
Make-up by: DePaul Norwood
Photography by: Patrina Anthony

ISBN: 978-0-9848556-2-9
ISBN-10: 0984855629

Printed in the United States of America

Table of Contents

Preface

Introduction

Day 1 – Choose ONE Focus	1
Day 2 – Small Steps	7
Day 3 – Have Faith	11
Day 4 – Expect Success	15
Day 5 – Good Habits	19
Day 6 – New Environments	25
Day 7 – Reflection	31
Day 8 – Positivity	37
Day 9 – Failure	41
Day 10 – Purpose Driven	45
Day 11 – DO Something	49
Day 12 – Life Defined	53
Day 13 – Obstacles	59
Day 14 – Stillness	65
Day 15 – Grateful	69
Day 16 - Let go!	73

Day 17 – Be Proud of your gifts   77

Day 18 – Choices   81

Day 19 - STAND in your POWER   85

Day 20 - KNOW your VALUE   89

Day 21 – A Plan for your Life   93

Just #DoBetter

Preface

There is no such thing as perfection. It doesn't exist. There, I've said it. Now that I've said it you can STOP chasing perfection and get STARTED because an imperfect start BEATS a perfect LACK OF STARTING any day of the week. Allow me to get deeper, if I start and perfect mine along the way, and you NEVER start because you are waiting on getting it just right, WHO will be able to help more people? Who will be able to cross the finish line? Who comes closer to walking in their purpose? It's the person who gets started, of course! Too many of you are WAITING to get things JUST right in order to get started and as a result you are MISSING the opportunity to get started at all. Just #DoBetter will help you do a little EACH day and challenge you to take SMALL and IMPERFECT steps because again, MOVEMENT is absolutely BETTER than being STUCK. Here are a few more things that you MUST know before you start this book.

Tomorrow never comes. Once the day that you are referring to as tomorrow arrives then guess what? It is NO longer tomorrow. It is not TODAY. So, for those of you who procrastinate please KNOW that there is nothing like doing SOMETHING TODAY. There is this thing called momentum and this other thing called consistency and those things will BLESS you if you continue to MOVE your feet daily even it's just if ever so slightly. The compound effect of moving your feet a little each day is much greater than waiting until ONE DAY and trying to fit it all in. Just

#DoBetter is going to challenge you to stay on the move until you have created a habit of movement versus a habit of procrastination.

Time is the same for everyone. If you are thinking that TIME will be better for you when your job is not as busy, or when your kids start school, think again. There was a song in the 70's (don't worry about how old I am!) that said "if it ain't one thing, it's another" and how very true that is. Even the bible says that IN this life there will be troubles so, waiting on the perfect time to start or thinking that you don't have enough time will cause your dreams to be lost to you forever. After all, WE don't know how much time we have on this earth. Tomorrow is NOT promised. STOP waiting on the perfect time or to have the time and create the time that is needed for you to pursue your dreams. Just #DoBetter contains steps that you can do in VERY little time each day. The question is, now that we have removed time as an excuse will you do them?

FEAR is not in control, you are. The more you are committed to moving EACH day the less there is to be fearful of. Take your life back from fear. You may be afraid of something that is WAY down the road. I am amazed by the things that I USED to be afraid of that are NOW some of my best assets and greatest accomplishments. Always remember that you did not get the spirit of fear from the creator. Fear is a human thing so, leave it with the humans. Stay prayed up and stay moving. I am not saying that the fear will go away, but somehow it becomes a little easier to work in spite of the fear when you continue down your path just ever so slightly each day. Just #dobetter and don't allow fear to steal your dreams.

There MAY be some other things holding you back that I didn't mention but the critical things in Just #DoBetter will get you started. This book is not a replacement for that OTHER book that has all of the answers, but THIS book WILL get you to moving IF you commit to reading AND act on what you learn daily! Ready to #DoBetter? Let's get started.

Dawniel Winningham

Introduction

"Small deeds done are better than great deeds planned"
– Peter Marshall

You have NO idea how excited I am to have you as a part of this challenge.

Purchasing this daily ACTION guide says a lot about you.

It says:

You are ready for change NOW.

You recognize the NEED to move forward in your life and/or business.

You are tired of being held back by FEAR or PROCRASTINATION.

You REALIZE that there is MORE abundance that you could or should have in your life

You are COMMITTED to taking SMALL steps each day to lead to the change that you are believing in GOD for!

Why 21 days?

It takes 21 days to form a habit and hopefully after 21 days of working with this guide you will have a penchant for taking action, a bias for movement and a thirst for moving forward. Each day you will have an assignment. Read it and ACT on it.

We are about to take advantage of some of the most powerful tools available as they relate to bringing about change.

Prayer. Simply put, prayer changes things.

Visualization/Mindset. Your MIND is where ALL change starts. Until YOU believe it, you cannot achieve it.

Action. So MANY people pray, but don't act. The bible was clear that FAITH without WORKS is dead.

Support. Don't keep this challenge to yourself. BE PROUD that you are seeking change. Talk about it on social media! Tell your friends and family. Use the hashtag #dobetter to tell about your results or to let people know that YOU are on a journey to improve YOU!

Day 1 – Choose ONE Focus

"A warrior is just an average man with Laser-like Focus."
– Bruce Lee

Just #dobetter

Rome was not built in a day and change is not made in one. For the purpose of THIS challenge choose ONE thing in your life and/or business that you want to focus on changing.

Many people get overwhelmed because they want to boil the ocean and try to change EVERYTHNG at once. The beautiful thing about this challenge is that you can ALWAYS start a NEW challenge NEXT month with whatever is keeping you stuck!

So, for now choose ONE area that you are in believing GOD to change in the next 21 days and Be Specific. Below are some examples:

Health: your ONE thing may be that you need to eat better DAILY and drink MORE water. I eventually want to lose 'X' number of pounds.

Finances: your ONE thing may be that you need to INCREASE the amount of money you have available so that you no longer live paycheck to paycheck. You eventually want to have at least 'X' number of dollars in the bank.

Business: your ONE thing may be that you need to generate MORE revenue in your business. You eventually want to be earning 'X' number of dollars each month in your business.

Career: your ONE thing may be that you need to shift your position at work OR need to find a new job. You eventually want to have a job earning 'X' number of dollars each month.

Relationships: your ONE thing may be that you need to create better relationships around you. You need to have a better relationship with 'X' person in the next 30 days.

These are just some examples.

What is the ONE thing you will focus on for the next 21 days?

Prayer

Each day pray a BIG prayer to GOD about the one thing that you are focused on changing in the next 21 days. Remember to pray BIG but ask GOD that HIS WILL and not YOURS be done. He may have a plan to help you that YOU have not considered.

For example:

Lord, give me the discipline when it comes to my finances to bring about a real change in my life. You have said that a wise man leaves an inheritance for his children's children. Help me bring about that level of abundance in my life.

Mindset/Visualization

Change happens in the mind first. Can YOU see yourself losing weight? Can you SEE yourself being a millionaire? Can you SEE yourself being three or four sizes smaller?

Spend at least 15 minutes today visualizing yourself the way that you WANT to be.

Think about ALL of the things that will be different.

If you lose weight, see yourself in new clothes. If you change your finances see yourself with money in the bank. If it's a new job, see yourself going to a new job each day.

Whenever you have a FEW minutes throughout the day say I AM, or I HAVE whatever it is you are working on. For example, I have a millionaire mind. I have plenty of money in the bank to help myself, my family, and my community.

Now ACT

This is where the work begins. What is ONE thing that you are going to do TODAY that is BOLD and will propel you towards your future? Below are some suggestions:

If you said HEALTH, take the opportunity to start a Food journal. TRACK everything you eat/drink for the next 21 days. BE RELENTLESS!

If you said FINANCES, start a finance journal. TRACK every dollar you SPEND for the next 21 days. BE RELENTLESS!

If you said business, start a REVENUE journal. Take a GOOD LOOK at what you are earning now and track DAILY what you are earning. After all, you are in business to earn revenue and you SHOULD be earning daily.

If you said RELATIONSHIPS start a gratitude journal. For the person you are working to build a better relationship with write down DAILY one thing you are GRATEFUL for them for. One thing they add to your life that you appreciate. (This will tell you quickly if you even need to pursue a better relationship with this person or cut them off altogether).

WHY are we tracking?

Up until now you may have IGNORED or AVOIDED whatever area it is that you would like to see change in. NO MORE! We are about to LOOK that THING in the face. Not just TODAY, but DAILY. In T Harv Eker's book the "Millionaire Mind", he says that small people have BIG problems, because they have NOT grown themselves. ALL people have problems, but when you grow YOURSELF then your problems shrink in significance.

Suggestion:

Get a notebook for this challenge or take advantage of the note section in this book and carry it everywhere. Start to write NOT ONLY your actions but your feelings, and even catalog your excitement about this challenge.

Success:

Completing THIS 21 day challenge is going to mean so much to your life. Even MORE than you can imagine right now.

Completing THIS 21 day challenge is going to break the spirit of FEAR, PROCRASTINATION, POVERTY and LACK in YOUR life.

This challenge is going to show you that YOU CAN accomplish WHATEVER you set your MIND to!

#DoBetter

I am praying for you, today and every day that you take the time, energy, and FOCUS necessary to take this challenge seriously, AS if your very life depends on it because it does.

I am touching and agreeing with you on this journey.

With MUCH love,

Dawniel

Dawniel Winningham

Day 2 – Small Steps

"Great things are not done by impulse, but by a series of small things brought together." -
Vincent Van Gogh

Just #dobetter

The first question I have for you is did you DO YOUR WORK yesterday? Remember, this challenge is as much about consistency and taking small steps EACH day as it is anything.

Today's focus is HOW BAD do you want it?

And what is **IT**?

Yesterday, I asked you to identify an area of your life that you want to change. We are not going to spend a LOT of time in the past, but we ARE going to THINK for a moment about WHAT has kept us from getting what IT is that we want.

Today we are going to NAME IT. Is it FEAR? Is it PROCRASTINATION? Is it TIME MANAGEMENT?

Prayer

Today, go to GOD in prayer ASKING that he help you REMOVE whatever barriers that YOU have internalized that are holding YOU back! We can't just keep saying LORD HELP! We have got to specify WHAT help we need from him or if we don't KNOW what help it is, just say LORD please help me with the problem that I am experiencing.

Visualize

Before NOW you may have made the problem BIGGER than the resolution. What I want you to do going forward is to visualize yourself as a warrior in full battle gear. Imagine yourself

FIGHTING what it is that you want to overcome and IMAGINE yourself winning!

How does it feel to finally lose weight? To finally get MORE customers in your business? To for ONCE have enough money to do the things that are important to YOU?

Whatever YOUR 'IT' for this challenge is, spend the time imagining that YOU HAVE conquered the battle!

Now ACT

Words may inspire but only ACTION creates.

Take ONE step today towards the 'IT' that you are believing in.

If you are believing in Weight Loss then read at least one or two articles today to motivate you AND complete your food journal. Make ONE change in your diet. Drink more water. What is the ONE thing that you are going to do?

If you are believing for Finances then what is the ONE thing in your past that has been sabotaging you? What are you going to do to correct it? Are you even aware of WHERE you are in your finances? Is it TIME to become MORE aware?

If you are believing for a change in your business or career, what does your step today look like? Will you start looking for a different job? Will you start calling more clients? What HAS held you back in the past?

Be Committed TODAY to take one step in the direction of your FUTURE! TRUST me, it's not easy, but it's worth it! Remember the GOAL for this challenge is completion!

Touching and agreeing with you on this journey.

With MUCH love,

Dawniel

#DoBetter

Day 3 – Have Faith

"Faith is not knowing what the future holds, but knowing WHO holds the future." – Unknown

Just #dobetter

Do you know what breaks my heart? There are SO many people in the world that are living at FAR less than what GOD desires for them. The major reason this happens is that THEY don't feel WORTHY of the abundance that GOD has ALREADY claimed for us!

I have NEVER seen SO many people that give up BEFORE they start and I have never seen so many people that allow their past, their mistakes or even what other people have told them to be the MEASURE of their worth.

THIS is NOT FAITH!

FAITH is seeing how GOD VALUES you! Seeing how GOD has forgiven you! Seeing that GOD said that he created YOU in HIS image.

That means your greatness is inherent. YOU were born with it but somewhere along the way you have allowed people to take it from you!

In this challenge I want you to TAKE IT BACK!

I want you to UNDERSTAND that you are WORTHY of WHATEVER success you are believing for in this challenge!

You are WORTHY of losing weight!

You are WORTHY of having a better job!

You are WORTHY of having a better business!

You are WORTHY of having a better relationships!

BUT YOU have to believe it first!

And then you have to ACT as if you believe it. Start putting yourself in situations in order to assert your worth.

Start telling YOURSELF daily and at every opportunity that YOU are worthy.

WORDS HAVE POWER! What you TELL yourself becomes true. CHANGE the conversation that you have with yourself and STOP having conversations with people that belittle, demean or don't believe in you!

GOD believes in you. HAVE conversations with him.

Prayer

Today when you go to GOD and when you read your Bible LOOK at all of the times that GOD says he loves you and that he wants the best for you. Look at all the times that he says that you are worthy, that you are gifted and talented. Would he lie? As you pray ASK for the courage to believe in WHAT he believes about you. Don't remember all of the bad things that you have done, remember that SALVATION saves us from having to pay the price for that. Amazing GRACE how sweet the SOUND that saved a WRETCH like me. Once you have PRAYED for forgiveness from your past then you don't have to relive it over and over. JESUS has already paid the price. Thank GOD for that and move on.

Visualize

Today visualize that YOU are a KING/QUEEN. Think of yourself as royalty BECAUSE you ARE! Remember who your father is? If GOD is the KING then all of us are princes and princesses. SEE YOURSELF sitting next to GOD. See yourself happy and being protected by him. Visualize people paying you compliments. KNOW that it is MORE than about how you look on the outside, but how you FEEL on the inside. Remember YOUR happiness is

YOUR job. Take time to SEE YOURSELF happy, not just today but every day.

NOW ACT

Do AT LEAST one BIG thing today that shows that YOU feel that you are worthy. EVEN if you don't feel it yet, you WILL if you keep doing this.

Go to a high dollar car dealership and test drive a car. Tell yourself that one day that car will be yours and even if you CHOOSE not to have it later, that you are WORTHY.

Go to a high end restaurant and have a cup of tea or coffee. While you are there hold your head high as if you DESERVE to be there, because you do. (If you are in Houston ask me about my Thursday trips to the Hotel Granduca, if you are not in Houston look up high end hotels in your city that may have happy hours, or tea time)

STAND UP to anyone or any situation that makes you feel that YOU are not worthy. Just because someone has more MATERIAL things does not make them better than you.

Write I am WORTHY so many times that your hand hurts! Say it out loud just as many times. Scream it at the top of your lungs.

Turn the TV off. STOP watching the things that make you feel as though you are not worthy. STOP listening to things that make you feel as though you are not worthy. Use that time instead to BUILD a WORTHY LIFE, one that you are proud of!

Remember THIS challenge is about consistency! Pat yourself on the back for the last three days and if you are just starting TAKE your time and let this sink in. THIS is the most important work you will do in your life.

Be Committed TODAY to take one step in the direction of your FUTURE! TRUST me that it's not easy, but it's worth it! Remember the GOAL for this challenge is completion!

Touching and agreeing with you on this journey.

With MUCH love,

Dawniel

_____
_____
_____
_____
_____
_____
_____
_____
_____
_____
_____
_____
_____
_____
_____
_____
_____

Day 4 – Expect Success

"Expectancy is the atmosphere for miracles." - Edwin Louis Cole

Just #dobetter

Are you LIVING a life of EXPECTANCY?

I LOVE when Joel Osteen opens his service and says, THIS is MY BIBLE! I am what it says I am, I can have what it says I can have, I can do what it says I can do.

Are you living your LIFE as if you can HAVE what the BIBLE says you can have?

Here are some things that the BIBLE says about abundance; There are really too many to list them all. After you read these the question is do you EXPECT for GOD to provide You with abundance.

John 10:10
"The thief comes only to steal and kill and destroy; I came that they may have life, and have it abundantly."

Isaiah 48:17
Thus says the LORD, your Redeemer, the Holy One of Israel, "I am the LORD your God, who teaches you to profit, Who leads you in the way you should go."

Ephesians 3:20
"Now to him who is able to do far more abundantly than all that we ask or think, according to the power at work within us,"

Ecclesiastes 5:19
"Everyone also to whom God has given wealth and possessions and power to enjoy them, and to accept his lot and rejoice in his toil—this is the gift of God."

2 Corinthians 9:8
"And God is able to make all grace abound to you, so that having all sufficiency in all things at all times, you may abound in every good work."

Prayer
Today you should PRAY expectantly. You should KNOW in your heart that GOD does not want you to have lack. KNOW that regardless of what you have done in the past that GOD has forgiven you and is WILLING to release the blessings to you, if YOU are believing. Remember the GOD that you serve. He said that HE can provide EVEN outside of the realm of OUR thoughts. Are YOU praying boldly enough? Are you ASKING for ALL of the blessings that he has coming your way, or are you asking for just enough to get by? Remember you get what you ask for, so don't be mad when the next person has MORE because they asked for more!

Vision
Today visualize yourself in abundance. See yourself with MORE than enough. See yourself paying bills on time and early. See yourself being able to provide seamlessly for yourself, your family and your community. SEE yourself being PAID well for the work you do in the world. What does that look like? More importantly WHAT does that feel like. Allow the feelings of BELIEF that THIS could be your life wash over you and RECEIVE the abundance that is heading YOUR way. Remember to picture it all! An abundance of Health, an Overflow of Money, Riches in Family and Friendship and ALL that life has to offer.

Now ACT

Today ACT as if abundance is on the way. Have a PLAN for the abundance that is coming. **Be BOLD enough to plan out your millions NOW!** How much will go to the bank. How much will be put aside for future generations? How much will go to specific charities in your community. Make this MORE than a fifteen minute task. Take your evening planning this abundance as if it is coming tomorrow. THAT is the power of belief.

If you are believing for weight loss, buy a pair of pants a couple of sizes too small. KNOW that you will be wearing them in the near future. SUCH is the power of belief.

If you TAKE your action seriously, the Holy Spirit will start to respond with abundance!

Touching and agreeing with you and your spirit of expectancy today and every day!

With MUCH Love,

Dawniel

Dawniel Winningham

Day 5 – Good Habits

"We ARE what we repeatedly do. Excellence then is not an act, but a habit." - Aristotle

Just #dobetter

If you have done every day of this challenge so far, it is no doubt that YOU FEEL the wave of change coming to you. I have heard from most of you by now and know that by executing these actions THINGS are shifting in your mind, body and spirit.

NOW is the time to make SURE that you stay on course. Things may pop up along the way that will try to distract you from getting this work done daily but commit to the process and not just for the duration of this challenge. LOOK for ways to continue to invest in and grow yourself LONG after this is over. THIS is only the start of WHO you can be and what you can become.

If your goal is to become a millionaire one day, it is said that it is NOT that you will become a millionaire that is the focus. Your focus should be the NUMBER of people you will have to serve in ORDER to become a millionaire.

The same is true with this process. DAY BY DAY improvement of yourself and the habits that you have will lead to a change in your lifestyle that makes virtually anything possible. YOU MUST stay the course and YOU MUST commit to the process.

This society has made us feel that things can be accomplished overnight. You and I both know that is not true. Stop allowing people to sell you the idea that success is anything other than a long, arduous, and complicated process. That is why you must have fun along the way and that is why you must do what you love. That is why you must be consistent day by day and that is why YOU MUST be committed to the process.

Too many people have just as much of a chance for success as the next person but, they do one of two things. They don't make the pursuit a habit, OR they quit before they have had a chance to be successful.

Don't allow these to be you. Continue these actions even after the challenge has completed. Feel free to go back and start another 21 days choosing a different focal point. This challenge is designed to be used over and over in different areas of your life. It is up to YOU how many times you use it and how much you use it to change your life. My suggestion is OFTEN and CONTINUOUSLY.

Prayer

It is ok to pray to the lord for stamina and it is ok to pray to the Lord for strength so, make sure that you do so with this challenge. CHANGE is never easy and sometimes our minds have a way of talking us OUT of doing the right thing. You must not allow it. You must ask GOD for the courage to change in order to pursue all that he has waiting on you. You must ask him for the strength to push past distractions and stay the course. All kinds of things will tempt you from this journey. YOU must not allow it. You must continue doing whatever you can over the next 21 days to make THIS journey a habit.

Visualize

Can you SEE yourself once you complete this 21 days? If you are someone who has the spirit of procrastination you should be patting yourself on the back EVERY DAY because You are doing it! You are showing up daily without excuses or distractions. You are getting things done NOW! Visualize the NEW you. One that people brag on for executing and meeting challenges head on. If fear is something you struggle with, visualize the brave NEW you, standing up DAILY for your gifts and talents. Ready to defend your destiny at all cost. Willing to invest whatever, Do whatever, and Learn whatever it takes for your life to be radically different.

If you are believing in a change for your health take time to SEE yourself once you have adopted a habit of daily good habits. See yourself jogging, drinking water, eating healthy. See the glow of your skin and the shine of your hair from taking care of yourself habitually.

Remember, Good habits build a good life.

Now ACT

Take accountability for your day from start to finish. What are the things that you are doing that are a waste of time or bad habits? Try to think of things that you may not have thought of previously.

As you catalog your day make a list of things that you would consider your GOOD HABITS and things you would consider your BAD HABITS. Be honest with yourself about the things you need to change. How many of them can you change with this challenge? Even if you need to take it over again.

Re-write your habit list. EVEN if you are NOT doing what you should NOW take EVERY bad habit and turn it into a positive.

For example, if you write down your bad habits list that you watch too much television write next to it that you watch VERY little television and that you spend at least 30 minutes each day reading and learning.

One of your bad habits may be the time you spend on the internet. Immediately start to limit yourself not just with the TIME that you spend on the internet, but WHAT you do when you are on there. We may both spend the same amount of time on the internet, however my time is spent earning. Your time may be spent idly or making plans for things you have yet to implement. Limit that idle time and spend MORE time focusing on what matters. Generating revenue, learning more, and being more productive.

The more you are able to start re-positioning your bad habits into good ones the more your whole life will change.

The reason that MOST people don't do this is because it never occurs to them. They are sleeping, living life however it comes to them. Living a life with whatever comes to them automatically as opposed to forcing change in their own lives. They don't realize the POWER that they have over their own lives, the POWER to change anything they don't like.

Don't be mad at the bad habits you have accumulated but instead work to replace them. Be deliberate and methodical in the creation of new habits.

Remember, this is a process. As long as you commit to doing the work then things will change. Your spirit may be fighting you but, don't give in. You accepted this challenge for a reason so, use everything in your power to push forward.

I am proud of you and rooting for your success.

Touching and agreeing with you for your stamina.

With MUCH Love,

Dawniel

#DoBetter

Dawniel Winningham

Day 6 – New Environments

"Surround yourself with people who LIFT you higher." –
Oprah Winfrey

Just #dobetter

Embrace NEW people, NEW things, and a NEW you! We are SO afraid about what people will say when we change that sometimes that keeps us from changing. We can NOT allow what people will have to say LIMIT us from improving our lives. In fact, we SHOULD seek new friendships, new experiences and be prepared for the NEW person that will emerge as a result of this challenge. I know it is cliché but I must use it because it is the perfect analogy. Right now, you are in a cocoon because you are only getting ready. The butterfly that emerges will be a result of the changes that you make NOW. As a new butterfly the worst mistake is to continue to hang around the caterpillars you were around before. Not only will they hate on your new beauty, but they will do their best to bring you down AND if you don't start hanging around butterflies, YOU are going to struggle with keeping your NEW butterfly mindset. You will start quickly forgetting how high you can fly. You will shift back into INCHING along the tree branches instead of FLYING through life, Get the picture?

Prayer
Pray to GOD today that he will start sending YOU new people in your life. He may have already started so, Be OPEN to what these NEW people can teach you.

The Bible says it repeatedly:

1 Corinthians 15:33
Do not be deceived: "Bad company corrupts good morals."

Proverbs 13:20
"He who walks with wise men will be wise, But the companion of fools will suffer harm."

The Bible even went as far as to say don't even EAT with them.

1 Corinthians 5:11
"But actually, I wrote to you not to associate with any so-called brother if he is an immoral person, or covetous, or an idolater, or a reviler, or a drunkard, or a swindler--not even to eat with such a one."

Visualize

Can you SEE yourself in RICH company? Can you imagine yourself being invited out to red carpet events or being invited to the white house? It is possible with the RIGHT associations. Recently, I was invited to be a special guest at a George Foreman fundraiser. I not only INVESTED to go, but I also purchased a table on behalf of my organization. I was able to meet the former heavy weight champion, the new Mayor of Houston and see some other powerful individuals in business that I would not have seen had it not been for my investment.

The point is, that these are all JUST people and you should be able to visualize YOURSELF among these people because we are ALL God's children.

I have received a proclamation from the Mayor of Houston due to my connections. I have received a letter from the Governor of Texas and a proclamation from the State House of Representatives due to my connections. I have received a

Congressional Letter and 3 Presidential Awards for community service due to my connections. Connections can take you to the next level REGARDLESS of who you are!

Now ACT

Don't underestimate the importance of this lesson. TODAY you need to take inventory of your friends and family. WHO are you spending the MOST time with? Are they helping you move to the next level? Are they challenging you to be your best? Sometimes we associate with the people whom life has connected us with naturally, friends, co-workers, family. These people probably LOVE you but they may not necessarily be the BEST people to spend your time with if you are looking to move ahead. Remember, people naturally tend to shy away from change and encourage others to do the same. Change for most people means DANGER and since they love you they don't want YOU in a dangerous situation.

However, YOU must take ACTION to remove yourself from the status quo. THESE connections may not come naturally but it is up to you to FIND and CULTIVATE these new relationships.

Remember the 6 degrees of separation? There is someone that KNOWS who YOU NEED to know in order to be successful. Question is, are YOU willing to build enough relationships to find out?

One of the reasons that I started The Wealthy Sisters Network was to be deliberate about finding likeminded men and women. First, so that this journey would not be so lonely and secondly so that I could leverage the skills of different people around me...and they could leverage mine!

I challenge YOU to not only join Wealthy Sisters Network (men are welcome) but I CHALLENGE you to get involved, networking, meeting people and building relationships. Take it a step further and be even MORE deliberate about networking by starting YOUR OWN CHAPTER in your community. It is a GREAT way to have the intentional next level connections you need to continue to grow. (Many of you have already joined, but if not consider joining us at wealthysistersnetwork.org or learn MORE about us by tuning into our telesummit. You can register at bit.ly/tweregistration2016)

Remember, THIS challenge is all about taking BOLD actions. Sometimes BOLD actions REQUIRE change and an investment in something different.

The other choice is that you can continue to live your caterpillar existence, and the truth is, who wants that when the butterfly life is so beautiful!

#Bethebutterfly

With MUCH Love today and every day,

Dawniel

#DoBetter

Dawniel Winningham

Day 7 – Reflection

"Dream. Believe. Do. Repeat." – Unknown

Do you feel your SOUL opening up?

If you have been committed to each day of this challenge then you SHOULD feel a shifting in your spirit. The last seven days may have caused you to confront some TRUTHS in your life that are not comfortable. There may have been some things in your life that you are just waking up to. There may have been some things that you may have been constantly lying to yourself about.

Some things that you realize NOW that MUST change in order for you to receive happiness and all that you deserve in this life.

The key realization may have been that it is 100% up to you to make this happen. I don't mean you have to do it alone, but I do mean that you have to take the first step. When you take the first step GOD takes five steps toward you but if you sit still in fear, he sits still also, waiting on YOU always to choose your path and waiting on YOU always to ask for the help that you need. So, if you decide not to ask for help, or you decide NOT to push forward, then you will JUST be allowed to sit and we all know that just sitting still is NOT going to move us to a life that we love.

So, if you have struggled this week, it's ok because that means that there are some things that you may have been avoiding to KEEP from being hurt. As long as you avoid those things, your soul can not be at peace.

But TODAY:

Rest, Reflect, Regroup

Today we will do as the Lord commanded and rest our minds. It doesn't mean don't do ANY activity, it means to shroud ourselves in the Peace that surpasses all understanding.

Prayer

Today pray for Peace and pray for GOD to help you with the turmoil that comes with facing the truth about yourself and your life. Pray for the support you need to continue on this journey and pray for the courage that you need to continue to look YOUR LIFE in the face and determine what needs changing. Pray for the stamina to make those changes and pray for the diligence to get up even after you may fall on this journey.

Visualization

SEE yourself at peace with your new life. Whether it is improved health, abundance, or living your dream it is important that you KNOW that this next journey is MORE peaceful than what you are doing right now. Right NOW you are fighting against your destiny and fighting against God's help. You are working harder to convince yourself that YOU DON'T deserve these things, but this challenge may be opening you up to the fact that YOU DO. So, today SEE yourself going along with Success peacefully. See yourself in your new place and how happy you are. See yourself as one with the Lord and with all that he desires for you.

Fill your mind with his abundance and his blessings as you prepare for another challenging week.

#DoBetter

Now ACT

Today I want you to spend some time writing and reflecting. If you have not been writing down your feelings each day, start to do so. Today write down some of the challenges this week and give yourself credit for how you have handled them differently than how you would have in the past. We won't honor the devil by saying that he is attacking us, instead we will tell the truth and acknowledge that each time we are faced with LIFE we have choices on how to handle what is presented to us. The truth is that sometimes we just make a wrong choice BUT grace saves us.

Celebrate the fact that you are on this journey and recommit to spending a minimum of 30 minutes to one hour each day to do what is required of this journey.

Celebrate the things that you have accomplished this week by taking action. Note that it wasn't as HARD as you thought it was, or maybe it WAS as hard but it was worth it.

KNOW that these small steps every day are powerful enough to lead you to where you want to be in life, business and everything else. There is a thing called momentum and THAT's what you are building by committing to this challenge each day.

Take today to be PROUD of yourself and realize that GOD is proud of you too, that he always has been, and always will be.

Write down at least 3 (but if you can come up with more keep writing) things that you have done this week to honor GOD, yourself, and your family.

I am so proud of all that you are doing and I know that GOD is honored as well.

Thank you so very much for allowing me to be a small part of this soul shift in your life.

With much LOVE always,

Dawniel

"One Day my Soul Just opened up" by Gemmia Vanzant

One day, my soul just opened up

and I decided

I was good and ready!

I was good and ready

to surrender my life to God.

So, with my soul wide open,

I sat down

wrote Her a note

and told her so.

-Gemmia L Vanzant

#DoBetter

Dawniel Winningham

Day 8 – Positivity

"Positive anything is better than negative nothing." - Elbert Hubbard

Just #dobetter

Today, focus NOT on what is wrong with this life, but what is right. Remember that complaining is negative energy, energy that you could be using to fix the problem.

When YOU are tempted to complain STOP and thank GOD for the life that you do have.

Start to look at the things you are tempted to complain about differently:

Ask yourself, is it something I can change? If so, then work on it.

Is it something that is out of my control? If so, then pray about it.

The faster we remember that GOD is in control the better off we will be.

I must admit that over the past few days I have been going through something personally and was so overwhelmed that I forgot to reach for God. There was absolutely NOTHING I could do about the situation but there is ALWAYS something that He can do about the situation, if nothing but to bring you peace about it. He gives us FREE will to change the things WE CAN control, and for everything else he gives us prayer, peace and salvation. Don't forget to use it.

Prayer

This used to be one of my favorite prayers;

The Serenity Prayer
O God, give us the serenity to accept what cannot be changed, the courage to change what can be changed and the wisdom to know the one from the other.

We must remember that in life there are things that can be changed, and things that are left up to the lord. Today, pray for the courage to change what you can (which should be plenty) and to accept with PEACE that only he can give, the things that cannot. The more you use this prayer, the more difference you will see in your life.

Visualize

Today, SEE yourself at peace. Whether that is on a beach, in the woods with a breeze blowing, or sitting in a chair in your backyard, what does peace look like for YOU? As you start to be able to visualize yourself at peace more and more, more peace comes to you. Shake off the turbulence of the world at least once each day and SEE the peace that you desire in your life. There is always a chance to have MORE peace in your life, but sometimes if you are not in a peaceful place it is hard for you to obtain. Take time to SEE your problems solved. Can you SEE yourself with more finances? Can you SEE yourself healthier? Carry this vision with you throughout the day and if you are tempted to complain about something that you can't change then take a moment to go to your place of peace and ask the Lord to meet you there. Remember if we visualize a journey as being HARD then that is what the journey will be. If we visualize a journey being peaceful, then that is what the journey will be. It is up to US and how we allow our minds to work to determine WHICH will be our outcome.

Now ACT

Here is the hard part, Make a list of things that you don't like about your life. Limit the list to five or ten things for now because you don't want to overwhelm yourself! Once you have completed the list go back and list next to each one whether you CAN change it, or whether it is IN GOD's most capable hands.

Those things that you CAN change, realize that THEY are the way they are as a result of your choices. REFUSE to complain about them and instead take the time to create an action plan for starting to change the things that you don't like.

For those things that are in God's hands remember the Lord works in mysterious ways, and that there is always a lesson in his actions. Commit to being open to receive WHATEVER it is that GOD is trying to tell you with his work, and refuse to use the energy to complain about the situation. Use that same energy to pray for clarity, courage and wisdom for the things you cannot change!

With MUCH LOVE and PEACE,

Dawniel

Dawniel Winningham

Day 9 – Failure

"Failure is an opportunity to being again, more intelligently." – Henry Ford

Just #dobetter

Please know there are NO Failures, Only Lessons Learned. Somewhere along the way we learned that failure was one of the worst things that we could do in life but the WORST thing that we can do in life is NOT TRY because that is failure within itself.

BE PREPARED to FAIL! Embrace it. Celebrate it. It may SOUND or FEEL weird but nothing changes unless you try and with trying comes some failure! The faster you FAIL the faster you learn.

Your business, your life, your health MUST be important enough for you to break outside of your comfort zone and try some things. You may not get it right the first time, but if you stay on the journey you will eventually get it RIGHT!

Think about something you have failed at doing in the past, instead of continuing to beat yourself up for the failure take a moment to think of what that FAILURE taught you! Without the MANY failures that we have experienced in our lives we wouldn't have even learned to walk!

It's time for us to look at failure differently. When we start to look at failure with excitement and with gratitude for what it is has taught us, we will STOP being so afraid to try new things. It is in the TRYING and having FAITH that we receive our rewards.

We also must STOP blaming (or giving credit to) the devil. It is sometimes through WRONG turns that we find the right way.

Prayer

Today, ask GOD for the courage to move forward and the strength to not only fall gracefully, but to get back up quickly. Today, we want to thank GOD for the failures in our life because they have taught us so much. We want to be thankful to him for the level of knowledge that ONLY comes through getting things wrong. Realize that the only failure is NOT finding and living up to God's purpose for you!

Visualize

This will be hard, but today visualize failure. Visualize starting something new and not getting it right but don't stop there. Visualize trying and trying, over and over again until one day you get it right and the flood gates of abundance open. Visualize how good you will feel that you stayed the course and did not give up. Visualize all of the times that you wanted to give up but GOD was in your corner and would not allow you to give up. Visualize how proud GOD will be that you found your purpose and that you lived it out.

Now ACT

Today, MOVE as if failure were not an option. Take a step forward that you have been afraid to take because you weren't sure. Accept the fact that it may or may NOT work the first time, but that you MUST applaud yourself for taking ACTION and having FAITH that it will work out because it will work out in one way or another. Either it will teach you a lesson that is mandatory for your journey forward, OR you will succeed. Either way YOU WIN! Failure is NEVER a loss, only a lesson.

You won't BELIEVE how much time you have been losing because you were afraid to act. Time is OF the essence. This life does not last forever. In the time you have spent contemplating how NOT to fail, you could have started, failed, started, failed, and started and succeeded. Stop counting yourself out because of fear of failure!

Now get to WINNING (or losing, which is still a WIN).

With MUCH Love,

Dawniel

Dawniel Winningham

Day 10 – Purpose Driven

"There is a great meaning in life for those who are willing to journey." - Jim England

BE Purpose Driven! People ask me all the time why am I always so fired up. Why am I always so motivated? How do I show up day after day excited and pumped up to execute?

It's simple.

I am driven by my purpose and I am POWERED by my God.

There was a time when I was driven by other people's purpose and other people's goals but that can only keep you excited for so long.

When you find YOUR purpose, the reason that GOD put YOU here on earth then you FIND a way to march towards that purpose daily, even if ever so slowly.

Being purpose driven also keeps you moving forward PAST distractions, PAST obstacles, and PAST other people's motives for you.

I guess you can sum it up in one word: Deliberate.

Today, think about everything you do and start to question- IS this moving me towards my purpose? Is this helping build on my purpose? If it is then do more of it. If it is NOT then remove it from your daily habit.

I will give you two examples of things that people may hate.

#1 is sales calls. Most business owners HATE to sell, but until you embrace it as part of the process your business will struggle.

Think about it, you could have the best product or service in the world, but if no one knows about it or if no one is convinced to buy it then it is all for nothing.

So, even though you HATE sales calls every call still moves you closer to your purpose. You may even want to consider doing more of them. In time, you may come to not only like them but to also be good at them and realize their purpose.

#2 is exercise. I personally HATE exercise but I have realized that if I don't exercise I won't be here to fulfill my purpose, so what can I do? I can do low impact exercise like water aerobics, or I can simply start to move more. Either way, it is a matter of KNOWING that in order for me to LIVE a purpose driven life I have to constantly be questioning my WAY and making sure that all of my time and actions line up with my reasons, my purpose.

Prayer

If you are not aware of what you feel GOD wants you to be doing in this life then pray. Pray without ceasing. Pray until you reach a conclusion. If you KNOW what GOD would have you do on this earth, then you need to pray today for the strength and stamina to see it through. It may not be easy, but WITH GOD you know it is possible. Seek His face for comfort when it gets rough and give the problems over to Him.

Visualize

Can you SEE yourself walking in your purpose? Can you SEE the confidence you have to know that you are HERE doing what GOD assigned you to do? Visualize yourself living a GOD approved life. What does that look like for you? I know that He has called me to serve millions so I must have IN MY HEAD what that looks like and KNOW that He is working with me to bring it to fruition. I know that HE can do all things and so I envision what that looks like. HOLD tight to the vision of your success today and every day. Remember, you don't have to have SMALL visions when you serve a BIG GOD!

Now ACT

I challenge you to keep track of ALL of your time today. What percent of that time was spent LIVING on Purpose? What percent of that time was wasted? Family time is living on purpose. Facebook for business is living on purpose. Television is NOT living on purpose. I am not saying you have to be 100% Purpose driven all of the time, life is still about enjoying the living, but at the same time, many people's top excuse for not making progress on their life goals is that they don't have time.

TODAY, know that you have TIME for whatever is important to you. So, if not having TIME to pursue your dreams or to build them is at the top of YOUR excuses list, cut that out now. If Beyonce, Oprah and Bill Gates have time, then you do too.

The question is, are you being purpose driven? Are you using your time deliberately?

Love you Much!

Dawniel

Dawniel Winningham

Day 11 – DO Something

"Knowing is not enough we must APPLY. Willing is not enough, we must DO!" - Bruce Lee

I don't know if you guys know how deeply personal each one of these messages are to me. See, each one of these messages are not just a message to you, they are also a message to myself. Think about it, you can't write without reading. The last few days I have had the blessing of hosting several fabulous speakers as they discussed their passions, what they love most and what they excel at in the world. Hosting these speakers quickly made me realize that I was at a deficit, not just for the things that I knew, but for the things that I was acting on.

Think about it.

We can have the world's greatest financial person deliver a speech about improving your finances and we probably know 80% of what they are telling us to do.

But do we do it? Are we WILLING to do it?

We may know that fast food is bad for us and that using credit cards will send us to debt purgatory, but are we willing to stop? Are we willing to do something different?

In our hearts, we may know that we NEED to start that business, write that book, or start that coaching program. We may KNOW that the world needs to hear our voice and we need to make a change in how things are going.

But we sit there.

We KNOW, but we are not WILLING.

Today, I encourage you to look at your life differently. What are you WILLING to do? What opportunities are you WILLING to say yes to? What knowledge are you WILLING to embrace?

When people start to tell me about how to lose weight I almost laugh internally, almost. It WOULD be funny except 80% of the things they tell me, I already know. Drink more water they say. Exercise more they say. Eat fewer calories they say. I know all of that. In fact, because my memory is so good I KNOW most of the calorie and fat content in MOST foods but until I am WILLING to put into practice what I know then it is just knowledge and the weight stays.

Same with you, until you are WILLING to do something different, nothing changes. It starts with being willing and the rest goes from there.

Prayer

Today, I am praying that GOD will move me from HAVING knowledge to being willing to use it. From KNOWING that I need change to being willing to ACT and bring CHANGE about. He says that faith without works is dead so, I know that I must be MORE than faithful. I must be in ACTION trusting Him to fill in the parts that I don't know. Asking Him for courage in the parts that I am unsure of. Allowing Him to lead me down the path of insecurity in order to reap the reward. I must place FEAR behind me and be willing to act so that I can claim the abundance that He has set aside for me already. Today, I pray to be a willing participant in my destiny. I pray that I say YES to activating the knowledge that is already in me.

Visualize

Today, SEE yourself being WILLING. I can SEE myself being willing to change my eating habits. I can SEE myself being willing to raise my rates EVEN if that means some people can't afford me. I can SEE myself still being heavily sought after and critically acclaimed. What can YOU see today as a result of YOU being willing. Being willing to say YES to yourself even if that means that you have to say no to someone else. If you are someone who ALWAYS says yes to others, (which may possibly mean no to you) then visualize yourself having the POWER to put yourself first and finally say no to others. Visualize YOURSELF saying YES to YOU!

Now ACT

Here is the scary part, now that you KNOW that you have been avoiding some things, or unwilling to embrace some things that are good for you, what will you do? Are you WILLING to say YES to those things even if they make you afraid and even if you KNOW that things will change and you are not sure how they will work out?

Today, write down FIVE things (I know that's a lot but this is a challenge, right?) that you KNOW you need to say YES to. Write down ONE step that you can take in order to say YES NOW to that thing that you have been denying.

It is AMAZING how things change when you confront yourself on paper, and guess what? I will be listing my five things and I will be TAKING action to make a difference in my life.

Will you?

With Much Love,

Dawniel

Dawniel Winningham

Day 12 – Life Defined

"Accept no one's definition of your life. Define yourself." - Robert Frost

Just #dobetter

Live LIFE by YOUR Design. So many people have given up their power. They have given up their power to choose the life they want and as a result they are living life by default.

ACCEPTING what is in their bank account as if there is no more money in the world.

ACCEPTING their weight as if it cannot be changed.

ACCEPTING the negative people around them as if positive people don't exist in the world.

Going about their day as if THIS is the life that GOD wanted from them.

I challenge YOU to CHALLENGE that notion.

Don't you think GOD wants you to be happy? Don't you THINK that GOD wants more for you? And if that is what you TRULY believe and think then the problem is YOU.

What are YOU DOING about changing your life? What are you doing to LIVE a life that you design? What are YOU doing to change your current situation to one that GOD has waiting for you?

If the answer is nothing or very little keep reading (even if the answer is something, keep reading).

The mind is a powerful thing oftentimes it acts like a sponge without wanting to or realizing it, it soaks up things in our environment.

We see thin people on television and they look happy so, we think that in order for us to be happy then we have to be thin.

We see rich people in the media and we think that that could never be us.

We see OTHER people living their perfect life, but because what we saw when we were growing up may not have been perfect, then we start to think that WE are not privy to that life but that is not true.

If GOD can do it for someone else then He can do it for YOU but YOU have to do the work. YOU can't just keep living life by DEFAULT. You MUST take the bull by the horns and start DESIGNING the life that you want to live.

Iyanla Vanzant says in her book that Thought + Words + Action = Results

Isn't that what we have been doing here?

Prayer – that is our thoughts; our conversation with God, but it can't stop there

Visualization – that is where we shape the words that we will speak about our life going forward. We have to see it in our mind first and then the correct words, more positive words, words that we were NOT speaking over our life start to manifest.

Action – Action is action. Once you have prayed and visualized YOU must get to work. YOU must meet GODS blessings at the door. He loves you and will give you whatever you ask for. You have got to REALIZE that in some cases you may have NOT been asking. You have just been accepting whatever came your way. In some cases you have not been visualizing. You were stuck in those same places that you were before without a New vision of your new life. You have NOT been acting in faith or abundance, you have been praying and then allowing the world to take over.

No More!

Prayer

Today pray to God for the consistency and the vision to DESIGN your own life. Regardless as to whether you feel that you are closing in on your ideal life or if you feel that you are light years away. Make it YOUR business to let GOD in on what you SEE for your life. If you can't see it then ask Him to send you mentors, coaches and accountability partners that may see MORE for your life than you can. ASK for the help you need to MOVE forward.

Visualize

HOW do you want your life to look? Vision boards are great but you need to learn to carry the life you design in your thoughts, so that when you see it in the world you KNOW this is the opportunity for you. Living LIFE by DESIGN means you have to KNOW what you want. Stop settling for small visions and stop associating with small minded people. The closer that others are to you that HAVE what you want, the more you will be able to hold on to the vision that YOU can also have this life.

Now ACT

Today, DESIGN your ideal life. I did not say perfect because I am not sure a perfect life exists. The Bible says, in this world you will have trouble. So, you will have trouble, but the greater you are at taking control of your life the smaller those troubles will appear.

What do you want your relationships to look like? What do you want your health to look like? What do you want your faith to look like? Your car, your house, your bank account and the others things that belong to YOU?

PUT this on paper and look at it daily, this is how you will know that you are coming within reach of the things that you are believing in GOD for. This is also how you are going to make it plain for HIM so that He knows what to bless you with.

With MUCH Love always,

Dawniel

#DoBetter

Day 13 – Obstacles

"Turn your stumbling blocks into stepping stones." - Unknown

Just #dobetter

Focus on OPPORTUNITIES, not OBSTACLES. We are going to talk about obstacles and opportunities from two perspectives today.

1. **Not being so focused on obstacles that you overlook the OPPORTUNITY**

2. **Missing opportunities because of perceived obstacles**

What are you focused on?

We grew up learning to view the glass as half empty or half full. Unfortunately, for many of us including myself, somewhere along the way we started looking at the glass as half empty. We forgot to LOOK for the opportunities and ONLY look at the obstacles. If you are NOT careful, a negative mindset will blind you from seeing the BEST in bad situations. That is how the mind is conditioned, however, it is time for you to recondition your mind.

It's time to SHIFT your focus. EVERY problem that is presented to you is an opportunity, remember that. Once you fix it, you have the OPPORUNITY to teach the world how YOU FIXED it and get paid for it.

Every Problem is an opportunity and every time you solve a problem it makes YOU stronger, so it is an opportunity to grow and learn.

Don't get caught up LOOKING at the obstacle, be grateful for the obstacle because it has given you an opportunity to grow.

Stop Missing opportunities. In fact, be in pursuit of them.

Opportunities are everywhere but sometimes you have to go and LOOK for them. I just sent two of my clients an OPPORUNITY to go to a free writing class for veterans. It is in another city and they have to pay their way to get there, but it is STILL an opportunity.

So, what are the obstacles?

They may not have daycare to watch the kids while they go. Figure it out.

They may not have the money to travel. Figure it out.

They may not be able to get the time off work. Figure it out.

STOP missing opportunities because of time, money, or any other reasons. Once you have prayed to ask God if this is the opportunity for you, allow NOTHING to hold you back!

I am constantly LOOKING for opportunities. Opportunities to be in the media, opportunities to grow my business, opportunities to win awards. If you don't look for them, how will you find them? Stop expecting that opportunity and blind luck will just show up on your doorstep. Be looking for them DAILY and you will be amazed at what opportunities you find.

Prayer

Today, pray to GOD to see the opportunity that may be hidden in your obstacle. Pray for Him to open your eyes to the lesson that comes along with each obstacle. Pray for the mindset to see EACH obstacle as a blessing and to be thankful in advance for whatever the current opportunity may reveal later. Last, but not least pray for the faith to endure the obstacle.

Visualization

What is an opportunity that you have now or that you have overcome in your life that other people are currently going through? Can you see yourself teaching the world how to overcome? Can you visualize people paying you to be the expert in that area? Or maybe it is a skill that you learned out of necessity? See yourself turning that skill into revenue and other people paying you for what you once thought was your obstacle.

Now ACT

Today, I want you to write down five obstacles that you have had in the past. You may still see them in less than favorable light. I want you to then write down five opportunities that have come as a result of those obstacles.

1. I got a divorce from my husband and that was an obstacle.

However, as a result, I went on to create my career as an entrepreneur. I would have NEVER come up on this opportunity had it not been for that obstacle.

2. I struggled financially when me and my husband split and that was an obstacle.

However, as a result of that struggle, I learned to generate revenue using MY skill and MY intellectual property.

Do you see where I am going with this? If I would have NEVER gone through the pain then I would have NEVER received the pleasure. Now, make your own list, and in the process start to see some things that have happened to you in the past in a positive light because THIS is how you move forward.

With MUCH Love always,

Dawniel

#DoBetter

Dawniel Winningham

Day 14 – Stillness

"Be Still and know that I am God." - Psalms 46:10

Just #dobetter

Today your ACTION is to do nothing. When is the last time you had that luxury? SOMETHING is always going on, and when NOTHING is going on we are fighting to make something happen but the most important thing we can do on this journey is to take time DAILY and if not daily at least once a week to be STILL.

> The stillness will restore you.
>
> The stillness will give you peace.
>
> You will find resolutions when you are still.
>
> God's greatness will reveal itself to you when you are still.
>
> Stillness will help you identify what is important (and what is not)
>
> Stillness will help you connect with GOD so He can order your steps.

So that when you do move, take action and take steps that your steps are fruitful as God would have them be.

THIS is what the Bible says about being still, If YOU are still, GOD will fight YOUR battles for you!

1. Zechariah 2:13 "Be still before the LORD, all mankind, because He has roused Himself from His holy dwelling."

2. Psalm 46:10-11 "Be still, and know that I am God! I will be honored by every nation. I will be honored throughout the world.

The LORD of Heaven's Armies is here among us; the God of Israel is our fortress." Interlude

3. Exodus 14:14 "The LORD will fight for you while you keep still."

4. Habakkuk 2:20 "The LORD is in His Holy Temple. All the earth—be quiet in His presence."

Prayer

Today pray for your mind, body and spirit to be still. Pray for GOD to take up whatever you are fighting WHILE you are still. We know that work is required, however there is much that can be done while we are still. We have to make sure that we hear from the LORD and we can only hear that still small whisper when we are STILL.

Visualize

Many people say that they STRUGGLE with being still. That there is too much to do, that they are not good at it. Whatever the case may be, the more YOU can SEE yourself being still and allowing the peace of GOD to wash over you, the more you can BE STILL.

Now ACT

DO whatever it takes to bring STILLNESS into your life. Even if it is gradual, once a week and then once a day. Do not forsake this peaceful time. PRAYER is when you talk to GOD. Being STILL is when you listen.

Write down what days and times of the week that you will be STILL. Guard these times as you guard your life. Do whatever it takes to make this time a habit. It won't be long before you yearn for this time when you miss it.

#DoBetter

Don't you WANT to know what GOD is saying? If so then be still.

With MUCH Love,

Dawniel

Dawniel Winningham

Day 15 – Grateful

Gratitude opens the door to the power, the wisdom, the creativity of the universe. -Deepak Chopra

Just #dobetter

Be GRATEFUL for what you already have and realize that what you DON'T have is YOUR fault. Allow me to be transparent for a moment (is there any other way for me to be?) I caught myself this weekend being Jealous! Being mad over something that someone else had that I didn't have and because I was too ashamed to talk to anyone about it the jealousy festered and grew and became obsessive.

And for what reason? Absolutely none.

I had a talk with my 20 year old son and he was like MOM, you're the bomb. You hold up this household, your kids, your mom, other family members and STILL ball out of control. You have built a dynasty in a few short years and you are ONLY 45!

That conversation reminded me of what all GOD has done for me. How far He has carried me and how far He has committed to carry me into the future. I immediately felt BAD for not being grateful for all that I do have.

The realization of it being MY OWN fault that I don't have what I think I should have caused a shift to happen.

Two things.

The fact my son is paying attention moved me.

The fact that I was allowing WHAT someone else had get in the way of me being grateful for what I have was crazy but after all I am only human.

Just like that the block was gone.

And two hours later I was able to put a plan on paper that will make me $600,000 (or more) in the next 12 months.

Not saying that to brag but I am saying that to ask YOU what opportunities are YOU missing because you have:

> Not done the work
>
> Not charged your worth
>
> Not realized your worth
>
> Been too busy watching someone else make moves
>
> Been too afraid to move forward
>
> Been procrastinating with your gifts

And the biggest question, WHEN will you stop and go get your money?

Prayer:

This morning I prayed to God to help me keep my eyes on HIM and not on the world. To keep my eyes on His gifts for me because they may look totally different than the gifts He has for someone else, but the abundance is all equal. I prayed that He continue to expand my territory and I let Him know that I am grateful, truly grateful for all He has done for me so far.

Visualization:

Today I am visualizing a different bank account, a different waistline, and a different ME. What will "the ME" that makes $1million each year look like. It is time for me to start seeing HER so that I can be her. Not only seeing her, but determined to see the people around her as successful. Yes, I could probably get there much quicker alone (or maybe not) but what's the fun in that. Besides, I see GOD requiring MORE of me in the future, so I best be ready.

Now ACT

What is your goal this month for revenue for your business? What are you going to do to bring it in? What are your health goals this month? Go ahead and put "IT" on paper today because that makes it real. Don't just put the goals, but back up the actions that are going to make those goals. What partnerships do you need? What steps will you have to take? I promise if you start NOW, "next month" will be one of your BEST months ever!

Keep fighting your inner-me (not enemy), I know I will.

With MUCH Love,

Dawniel

Dawniel Winningham

Day 16 - Let go!

"Accept what is, let go of what was, and have faith in what will be." - Unknown

Just #dobetter

How many things in your life would improve if you simply LET GO?

Many of us are holding our dreams hostage with made up stories about success or how we can't have any or that it is not for us. What if we were to LET go for once? Risk it all? Maybe we will fail but maybe we won't.

Sometimes we have to LET GO of old habits, old friends, and old places. Even though they make us comfortable they also keep us stagnant. We have to decide that we would RATHER have a better future than a comfortable past.

Sometimes we have to LET GO of our thinking. That same thinking that got you HERE will not carry you to the next level. We have to be the FIRST to realize when our thinking is WRONG, when we are lying to ourselves or when we have just been taught the wrong thing in life and LET IT GO.

You MAY even have to LET GO of yourself. What WOULD you do if you only had six months to live? What would you do if failure weren't an option? What would you do if money weren't a concern? Whatever YOUR answer to that is, then find a way to do it NOW.

Years ago I recognized that the person I was BORN to be and the person that I was THEN could not occupy the same space. I had to CHOOSE did I want the NEW me or to keep the OLD me. I am SO glad I CHOSE to let go.

What will YOU do?

Prayer

The BIGGEST part of letting go is having the faith that GOD will catch you. You may think back to the past where you may feel that GOD did not catch you. However, if you made it HERE in some shape, form or fashion it may have been MEANT for you to fall. Today PRAY for the faith to LET GO. KNOW that GOD will send you the parachute, safety net or whatever else you need for you NOT to fail. Know that sometimes FAILING moves you closer to success and pray that GOD give you the stamina to get back up and try again, EVEN after you fall. Now THAT is faith!

Visualize

Think about how wonderful it would be if you let go. TODAY, take the chance to visualize HOW FREE you would be and feel if you let go. How much could you accomplish if you STOP being afraid and STOP procrastinating and let go? How much would you earn if you STOPPED holding back and STARTED charging what you are TRULY worth? SEE yourself letting go today and step into that feeling.

Now ACT

Now, here comes the hard part. Name at least one (or three if you are brave name) thing that has been holding YOU back. THINGS that you need to let go of but don't stop there. Set a date that you will let go of these things. If you are really bold and bad tell other people or even hold a virtual or in person party to celebrate their departure.

#DoBetter

It is UP to you to identify and REMOVE those things that are keeping you back. EVEN if it is your INNER self!

With MUCH Love,

Dawniel

Dawniel Winningham

Day 17 – Be Proud of your gifts

"The meaning of life is to find your gift; the purpose of life is to give it away." – Pablo Picasso

Just #dobetter

STOP Apologizing for Progress!

We grew up hearing, speak only when spoken to. We grew up thinking that NO ONE wanted to hear from us, and that no one wanted to be a part of what we were doing. Somewhere along the way we started trying to DOWNPLAY our gifts and our talents.

> So People wouldn't think we were bragging.

> So People wouldn't think we were trying to be better than them.

> So People wouldn't feel bad that WE have something that they didn't.

The time for that is OVER! It is time to STOP downplaying what GOD gave you and to WALK unapologetically into YOUR SEASON.

What is STOPPING you from TELLING the world, how GREAT GOD made you. The only answer to that is YOU and until you get COMFORTABLE allowing the GLORY of GOD to shine through your gifts...

You will keep feeling like something is missing.

You will keep allowing abundance to be something that other people have.

You will STAY trapped in your pity and sorrow.

GOD gave us all gifts and the amount of the GREATNESS that we pull from these gifts are up to you.

I am an excellent speaker, a great writer, a terrific motivator and an awesome coach and guess what? I am NOT sorry for it because GOD made me this way. What has GOD done for YOU that you are scared to show the world for FEAR of what PEOPLE may say? STOP worrying about what people have to say and worry MORE about what GOD is saying about you NOT using your gifts.

Prayer

Today, GO TO GOD in prayer and thank Him for the many gifts that He has given you. Thank Him for the obstacles because they have taught you. Thank Him for the trials because you have learned from them. Thank Him for the gifts that you use and the ones that you don't use. Recommit to finding GOD'S purpose for your gifts and ask GOD to show you where they are located and how you can USE them more!

Visualize

Visualize the day that GOD bestowed gifts upon you. What did He expect you to do with those gifts? What was the conversation like between you and Him? What POWER did He give you to operate in those gifts? SEE yourself living in your gifts unapologetically. You NEVER have to apologize for what GOD has done for you.

Now ACT

Think of THREE people that you are hesitant to share your greatness around them or with them. I challenge you to have a conversation with them about WHAT GOD is doing in your life and do so unapologetically! Even if THEY don't receive the conversation well, remember that YOU have the power to MOVE forward EVEN if you don't receive their approval and KNOW next time NOT to look to them for approval when you have so many others who will greet what you are doing with open arms.

Part 2 of the challenge:

Stop HIDING your story because your story was given to you FOR you to overcome and THEN share with the world. I challenge you to join me in my next book opportunity and SHARE your story with others who may be going through the same thing. Complete the application below NOW and STOP being afraid to SHARE what GOD gave you, EVEN IF and ESPECIALLY if, it is your obstacles. Somebody, somewhere is waiting to HEAR from YOU!

Today's Reading?

Why YOUR STORY of course! Make it a habit of making a list of your accomplishments and patting yourself on the back for what you have done great! YOUR story matters, NOT just to you, but to others as well. Tell it EVERY chance you get.

With MUCH Love,

Dawniel

Dawniel Winningham

Day 18 – Choices

"We all create the person we become through choices." - Eleanor Roosevelt

Just #dobetter

Remember Choices are YOURS; (You have them)

> YOU choose where you work

> YOU choose where you live

> YOU choose your friends

> YOU even choose the quality of YOUR life

> YOU even CHOOSE how much YOU want to earn

So where you are NOW is a result of YOUR choices? NOW it's time to make some new ones. What you do TODAY changes everything and gives you an opportunity to redirect your life.

STOP choosing what you think others want you to choose.

STOP choosing what you feel is best for others.

START choosing with your heart and with your mind and with your eyes on what GOD wants you to do.

If you are NOT choosing then you are living your life by default. People think that if they don't choose then they don't have to worry about failing!

WRONG answer. **If you don't CHOOSE then whatever happens to you is STILL a choice and if you are not doing ANYTHING you are STILL failing!**

Prayer

Thanking GOD today for FREE will and the ability to make CHOICES. Asking for WISDOM to make the RIGHT CHOICE and knowing that NOT making a choice is NOT the right choice. Praying for the courage to make BOLD choices today and to stand by them.

Visualize

Can you SEE yourself choosing to LIVE differently? Taking advantage of the choices that you have EVERYDAY? Are you ready to leave your job? Then SEE yourself CHOOSING to do so! Are you ready to have a FULL bank account? Then SEE yourself CHOOSING to build your business. Visualize yourself making choices BEYOND fear and those things will start to come to you.

Now ACT

WHAT are some CHOICES that you are making (or not making) that are contributing to your current life? Think of the choices that are causing you to have a life that YOU are not happy with. Write down at least THREE and a date by which you will CHOOSE to do differently.

Are you CHOOSING to be overweight?

Are you CHOOSING to stay in a relationship that doesn't make you happy?

Make SURE you include at least THREE other choices you COULD make. For example:

I am choosing to stay at a job where I am not happy:

I could CHOOSE to get another job.

#DoBetter

I could CHOOSE to look for another job within the company.

I could CHOOSE to leave and start my own business.

CHOICES sometimes require that we LOOK at the situation and acknowledge that WE are in control and ask ourselves now WHAT are WE going to do about it! Remember, we can make CHANGE or we can make CHOICES but excuses are OUT of the question.

With MUCH Love always,

Dawniel

Dawniel Winningham

Day 19 - STAND in your POWER

> "The past cannot be changed. The future is still in your power." – Hugh White

Just #dobetter

You have it, you know, we all do. It doesn't matter if you are shy or if you are an extrovert, I am talking about standing in the

> POWER that GOD gave you.
>
> POWER to live your dreams.
>
> POWER to stand up for yourself.
>
> POWER to Choose.
>
> POWER to take back your life!

Are you ready?

Have you given your power over to others by not charging your worth? Have you given your power over to others by not living your dreams?

When you PUT what is important to OTHERS in front of your dreams *and not just on occasion, repeatedly, YOU are giving away your POWER.

When you don't MOVE because of FEAR you are giving away your POWER.

When you put off doing the things YOU KNOW that you should be doing, you are giving away your POWER.

When you spend your money without thinking, when you eat those things that keep you heavy, when you fight with your family for no reason, when you say negative things TO yourself, about yourself, you are GIVING AWAY your POWER.

STOP acting helpless and remember who your Father is. EVEN when things get hard LEAN ON HIM and expect Him to DO what He said He will do and that is keep you on this journey. Remember that with Christ ALL things are possible.

So, when you have a moment and you start not to believe in the POWER that HE has given you, take that same moment to REMEMBER HIS power. If you can't stand in your own, then at least stand in His!

Prayer

Today, go to GOD in prayer asking Him to restore YOU with the power that He has given you. ASK Him to SHOW you the many sources of POWER that you have access to through Him. Ask Him to continue to hold you up and keep you but most of all give you the COURAGE to stand in WHO He created you to be. Time to STOP hiding your greatness and TIME to STAND in your power!

Visualization

Think of yourself standing tall. Visualize yourself in a confrontation with your biggest fear. Think of yourself as how David stood facing the giant. See yourself picking up five smooth stones and using those stones to knock YOUR giant out. WHATEVER your fear is make sure the giant has on a shirt with the name of your fear on the front so you KNOW who you are fighting. How does it feel to use the slingshot to beat the giant? How does it feel to know that GOD will not allow you to fail? How does it feel to hear the roar of the crowd as you overcome your fears! HOW does it FEEL to be powerful?

Now ACT

Name ONE thing you have been afraid to do. Take back your power and do it, ASAP.

If it will take more than a day, make a plan to accomplish your fear over the next five days. Is it a call you have been dreading? What book have you been thinking about writing? What business have you thought about starting? START NOW! You will be blessed by your decision to LEAP into your POWER.

We are coming to the finish line...no more hiding behind these words. We have been building up for the last 19 days, so you should be MORE prepared and be able to see MORE clearly than you were initially. Time to MOVE, MOVE, MOVE!

With MUCH Love,

Dawniel

<u>Today, WRITE your OWN story.</u>

Dawniel Winningham

Day 20 - KNOW your VALUE

"Don't let someone who doesn't know your value, tell you how much you're worth." - Unknown

Just #dobetter

Somewhere along the way we have forgotten our value. The value that GOD assigned to us is PRICELESS but yet we operate in the world as if we have NO value.

As if OUR JOB assigns our value – We associate our value with our worth at our places of employment.

As if the WORLD assigns us our value – We associate our value with what other people have to say about us or have said to us

As if OUR partners assign us our value – We associate our value with what our boyfriends, girlfriends, husbands and wives have to say about us.

WHAT ABOUT what GOD has to say about us? What about being fearfully and wonderfully made?

That being said our EARNING potential is UNLIMITED. WE must know our value and LOOK for the value in what we do each day. If we are unable to identify with and put a price on our value we will continue to struggle for abundance in this world.

Prayer

Today PRAY to GOD and thank Him for the blessings that He has heaped upon you. Thank Him for even the obstacles, because they have taught us something. Thank Him for His continued support and grace and thank Him for the challenges that He has led you through, because each of those challenges were a stepping stone to your greatness.

Visualization

Today envision yourself being VALUABLE. SEE yourself receiving six-figure checks and ENVISION yourself being highly sought after for the skills that GOD gave you, so much so that you are turning down opportunities. Imagine the greatness that GOD has waiting for you and how your life will be different when you LEARN your value.

Now ACT

Read this article...THINK about the things that you do that you are NOT translating into abundance http://time.com/money/3849100/what-mom-is-worth/

Look for VALUE in your skills – Are you a good cook? Are you a great resume writer? What skills/value do you have that you can convert into abundance?

Look for VALUE in your knowledge – What do you KNOW? Are you an expert in accounting? Are you the best at sales? What KNOWLEDGE do you have that can be converted into abundance?

Look for VALUE in your obstacles – What has held you back in the past? How did you get over it? Are there others who are going through the same thing? What obstacles have you overcome that you can convert into abundance by helping others?

#DoBetter

Make a LIST, put a price on them, and get to work operating in the abundance that GOD has given you.

With MUCH Love,

Dawniel

Dawniel Winningham

Day 21 – A Plan for your Life

> "Why don't you start believing that no matter what you have or haven't done, that your best days are still out in front of you." – Joel Osteen

Just #dobetter

God Loves You and wants the best for you!

It's as simple as that. Since GOD loves you, it is imperative that YOU love yourself. LOVE of yourself translates into a lot of different things:

1. You MUST forgive yourself for the past

2. You MUST take care of yourself Mind, Body, and Spirit

3. You MUST take time for yourself to restore yourself and honor yourself

4. You MUST make YOU a priority

Even days that I am not 100% happy with myself I remember that GOD loves me, and if GOD loves me, then who am I to NOT love myself.

Loving myself means:

Having confidence in my abilities

Having strength to overcome my fears

WANTING to move to the next level in life and not just staying where I am

Appreciating WHAT I have to offer the world, and not letting the world make ME think that I don't have anything to offer

I know it sounds easy, but in today's world it is actually quite difficult to remember just HOW MUCH you are worth and JUST how much GOD loves you.

But know THIS, EVERYTHING is working together for your good.

Every obstacle is for a reason; Even the places you can't stand are teaching you something. When you realize JUST how much God loves you, you will realize that your obstacles are only temporary lessons. KNOW that He loves you and RISE above the turmoil!

Prayer

Today pray thanking God for His love and for His protection. Pray asking Him to SHOW you your greatness and give you the courage to walk into it. Pray asking Him to SHOW you how to forgive yourself and move forward.

Visualize

Can you SEE yourself as GOD sees you? Just imagine how you look to GOD and WHO he created you to be. Spend the day visualizing yourself being surrounded by the love of GOD. Acting as if YOU were created in HIS image (because you were) KNOW how much differently that will allow you to operate and what a difference that will make in your life.

Now ACT

Write yourself a love note as if it came from God. Be sure to include versus from the Bible that reflect the love God has for you and the power he has given you. Hang the note somewhere where you can reflect on it daily. (Even consider having it framed)

#DoBetter

NEVER forget how much GOD loves you and wants the best for you. EVEN when (and especially when) things get touch, ask yourself, what is the message? What is GOD trying to tell me?

With MUCH Love,

Dawniel Winningham

www.ingramcontent.com/pod-product-compliance
Lightning Source LLC
Chambersburg PA
CBHW050654160426
43194CB00010B/1934